This Book Belongs To

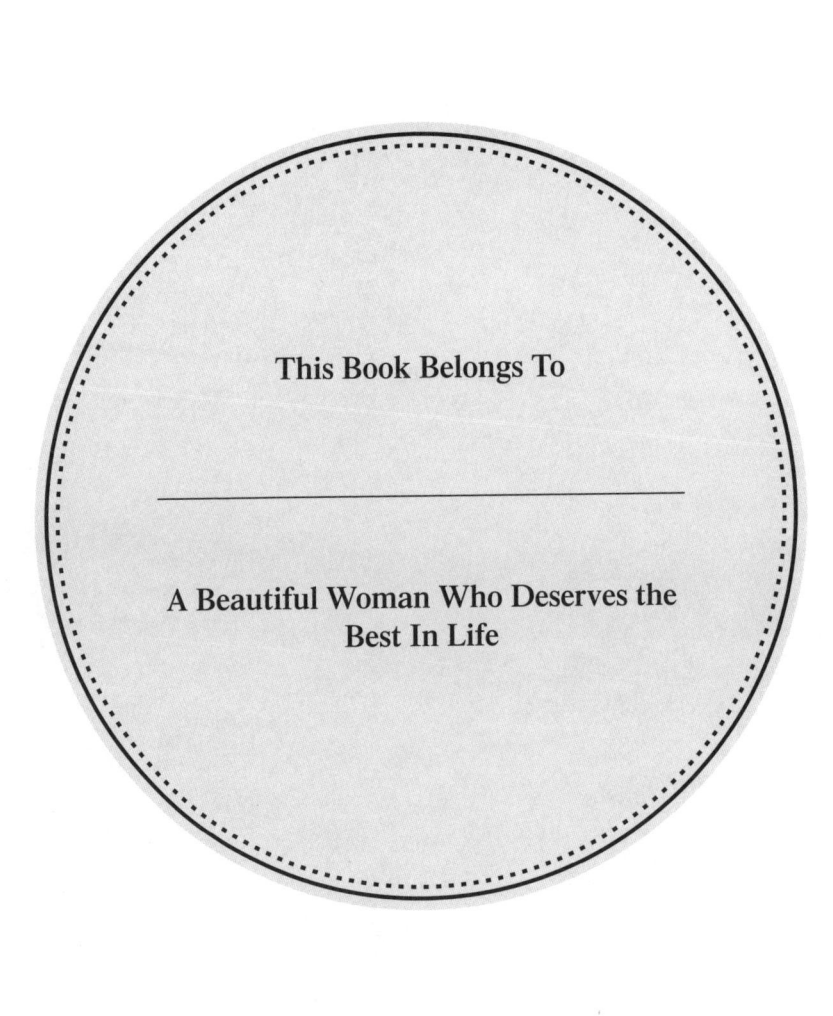

_____

A Beautiful Woman Who Deserves the
Best In Life

Dedication

To Quinn and Jameson

The Loves of My Life

How To Survive In The 21st Century as a S.S.O.F.F.*

*Suddenly Single Over Forty Female©

By
Rita Lee Lloyd

Illustrated by
Mary Ann Browning Ford

How to Survive in the 21st Century as a S.S.O.F.F.*
*Suddenly Single Over Forty Female©

Published by:
Dappled Sunlight Publishing
P.O. Box 3120
Dana Point, California 92629
www.dappledsunlightpub.com

ISBN# 978-0-9836498-0-9

Copyright © 2011 by Rita Lee Lloyd
Printed in the United States of America

No part of this publication may be reproduced, stored in a retrieval system, or transmitted in any form by any means – electronic, mechanical, digital photocopy, recording, or any other without the prior permission of the author.

All rights reserved solely by the author. The author guarantees all contents are original and do not infringe upon the legal rights of any other person or work. No part of this book may be reproduced in any form without the permission of the author. The views expressed in this book are not necessarily those of the publisher.

Table of Contents

PROLOGUE		13
FIVE BASIC RULES!		
1	Learn to Take Care of You!	19
2	Keep Your Sense of Humor!	43
3	Date at Least One Younger Man!	57
4	Never Give Your Real Age!	67
5	Live With Finesse!	79
EPILOGUE		89
ACKNOWLEDGEMENTS		93
ABOUT THE AUTHOR		95

Prologue

What is a SSOFF? She is a woman who was married or in a committed relationship for at least several years and believed it would last forever. She enjoyed the *wife and mother, SUV and Golden Labrador* lifestyle. She wasn't subservient to anyone; she was educated, capable, interesting, productive, creative, and basically happy. Then, seemingly out of nowhere, that *lifestyle* changed. Her husband/partner, whether through *death or disinterest*, was gone.

I really dislike labeling. However, in our current American society, labels are a fact of life. People can and will be labeled. Business woman, homemaker, stay at home mom, working mom, divorcee, widow, to name a few; labeling is a quick and easy method to refer to one's status and can be useful at times. Unfortunately, most of us buy into our labels and when they change drastically, we can be devastated.

Rita Lee Lloyd

The SSOFF is *not* a female Donald Trump, a driven career woman, or a woman who is *totally* happy being *totally* on her own and in charge of everything. Without apology, the SSOFF enjoys caring for others and being cared for. While completely capable of running the show by herself, she just never wanted to. Sharing her life, her love, the ups and downs of living with someone was a choice she made – and was good at. She may have worked outside of the home, had a career, been a CEO or celebrity. But her #1 priority was her home and family. I could go on and on as to the reasons why she chose this lifestyle, but in the interest of brevity, I won't (I know – too late).

Simply stated, through no deliberate choice on her part, the SSOFF's life turned upside down quickly and completely. It happened to me several years ago and I'm still living in a parallel universe. I want to share my discoveries, and those of my friends with other SSOFF's in the hope that I might make the transition to whatever lies ahead just a little easier, or to at least let you know you are not alone!

Rita Lee Lloyd

Five Basic Rules

Rule #1

Learn to Take Care of You!

The most important rule and possibly the most difficult –

I'm still working on it!

Easier said than done!

When I became a S.S.O.F.F. and people first said to me, "but now you have time for yourself," I just kind of went "phhhtttt." I didn't need any more time to myself. This *time* I already had – it was lonely, it was empty, it wasn't any fun. But *now I get* what I was supposed to be hearing at that point – that I had time to *learn* about myself. To really get in touch with *me,* the person I have always been, the person I'm growing into, the person I am destined to be. Learning about myself was vital.

Regardless of how you were in the past – you *have* changed. God, the Universe, whatever you believe gives us life, has said, "Here is where you are today – live with it!" And again, regardless of your beliefs, knowing who you are at this moment is the first step to survival.

> *... knowing who you are at this moment is the first step to survival.*

When newly single, it is very easy to overreact either in an extremely conservative way or an extremely bold way. And candidly, you don't want to do either one. Avoid the Birkenstocks, baggy sweats and scrunchy. By the same token, don't run out, get tattooed, and buy thong underwear and a navel ring, at least not yet. It's really important when you're first in this state of disbelief to maintain a balance. I realize that a sense of balance comes easier to some than others. This can be a very difficult area to master, but make it your goal for now. It will be well worth the effort.

As a S.S.O.F.F. it is time to focus on caring for yourself. A big part of caretaking includes the physical as well as the emotional aspect of our lives. Though it's more than four letters, the "E" word has always been abhorrent to me, something to be avoided at all costs! I'm referring to "exercise" of course!

However, I will be the first to admit that it is a necessary evil if I want to remain in good health and control my stress level. I've always admired you women who make exercise a part of your daily regime. You already have a "leg up" on being good to yourself. As for me, I have chosen a simple thirty minute walk at least five times a week as my concession to this requirement. And if pressed, I *will* further admit, it makes me feel like I am really doing something good for *me*! Sometimes I even look forward to it – go figure!

Keep your Glass Half Full!

Everyone has heard the question used to determine if you are naturally optimistic or pessimistic: "Is the glass half full or half empty?" It will come as no surprise that studies have shown people with a more optimistic outlook are healthier and happier than those with a pessimistic attitude.

> . . . studies have shown people with a more optimistic outlook are healthier and happier than those with a pessimistic attitude.

An article in *Parade Magazine*, by Dr. Ranit Mishori, covered a recent study of 100,000 women over an eight year period. The conclusion? Optimists had a 16 percent lower risk of heart attacks. In 2000, a Mayo Clinic study following pessimists over a thirty year period showed they ran a 19 percent higher risk of early death than optimists! Many other studies have proven a link between optimism and good health.

I'm not advocating an unrealistic pie in the sky attitude. And an honest "this really sucks" expletive uttered occasionally never hurt anyone. However, prolonged viewing of a half empty glass can definitely be detrimental to your health!

Our society has a template for an *acceptable timeframe* for grieving. If widowed, it's approximately two years; if divorced, it's much shorter – like, "the papers are signed, what are you waiting for?" I personally found it extremely difficult to remain optimistic about my situation after the initial acceptable period of grief had passed. Once the formal grieving was over, the realization that "this is my life" really set in.

Even though being optimistic had always been my method of operation, my light at the end of the tunnel wasn't remotely visible. In fact, the tunnel that had become my life was dark and suffocating. But, I realized very quickly that I could not allow myself to wallow in the comparative feeling of safety the darkness provided, or I would be in danger of losing myself.

Humans, by nature, are social animals. We fare much better with moral support given and received. Therefore, if your glass isn't at least creeping up toward the half full level, you may wish to seek professional help. Some of us may have a terrific friend network that provides the moral support we desperately need. However, as I found out, an objective therapist can offer *tools* as well as support. Realizing you need to improve your emotional state is one thing – knowing *how* to do it is another. If you need help keeping that glass half full, then get it! Believe me, even your BFF's will appreciate it.

> Realizing you need to improve your emotional state is one thing – knowing how to do it is another.

(Re)Create Yourself

Okay, so at the risk of contradicting myself – I'm going to address the issue of labels. While I *really do* hate the idea of buying *into* the labels "they" have given me, I am *all for* labeling myself. By that I mean – how *I* see me, how I want to *be* seen. My *own* self-image, my *own* label.

For several years, as wife, mother, homemaker, etc., you justifiably took pride in these titles and presented yourself accordingly. Now, while you may still be many of these, except for wife, the dynamic is different. If you're a mother, that won't change and motherhood will remain a priority.

However, mother or not, other positions you fill will reprioritize themselves. Career Woman – you may go back to work, or continue working; Chairperson, Volunteer – you may decide to join new groups; Divorcee, Widow, Hot-Mama – you most certainly are going to rejoin the singles scene, even if reluctantly. All of these personas will present an image – one which *you* must and will determine!

The labels have been around forever and will continue to be. But you *do* have a choice over the image your label projects. Merry Widow, Gay Divorcee, Soccer Mom? Sure, these are clichés. But they create an image that accompanies a label.

Rita Lee Lloyd

I would *never* have believed that *my* self-image needed a change! When I was in my comfort zone as the secure and happy wife, my self-image was intact. However, when the sudden change in my status occurred, so did my self-image. Sudden changes can create emotional upheavals that have little basis in reality. Hence – your self-image can become skewed beyond recognition, as mine did.

I found myself in that parallel universe where the *me* that had been, was not the *me* in the mirror. Did the reflection represent how I was feeling, or how I wanted to feel? Well, the person in the mirror was feeling like %*#$! And that wasn't acceptable. If the old me was no longer *acceptable*, change became inevitable. And I determined that with change, the new me would be *terrific!*

You may be thinking, "The last thing I want to do right now is create a new image – I'm not through with the old one." I understand, I never said this would be easy, but it *is* a necessary part of your survival. Besides, if you've gotten this far, you've done the hard part, the *change* has already begun.

I have found the quickest way to "inner change" is to begin on the outside. You know the adage, "Smile, it's difficult to be sad when your face isn't." Back in our mother's and grandmother's day, ladies bought a new hat to lift their spirits. For me, it's usually a new purse; weight gain or loss hasn't affected my purse size. But admittedly, you are not simply down in the dumps, you are devastated! So. . . it's going to take more than a new hat

> "Smile, it's difficult to be sad when your face isn't."

or bag to improve your feelings and your image. Therefore, I'm going to *try* and make this as simple as possible – your job is to make it *fun*!

Finding the Right Image

I've always believed that first impressions *last!* Normally, the first thing you do when meeting someone new, is look at them. Whether at the store, an office, a gala, or other event, you get a lasting impression of a person's physical presence before they even speak. And let's face it – we all form opinions of someone based on how they look. "People watching," anyone?

Quickly – describe someone you know well using five adjectives only. "Attractive, energetic, intelligent, friendly, dynamic." I have just described a good friend I've known for years. If you were in a roomful of strangers, you'd probably be able to pick her out based on my description. She radiates these qualities both in her manner and in her dress. Her image beautifully represents who she is.

Now, find five adjectives describing *you*. (Notice I didn't say quickly?) To find the perfect adjectives to best describe *you* will take some thought – maybe a *lot* of thought! You're looking for words that fit the *you* who is rising from the ashes of emotional turmoil. The "new and improved" version that will speed you happily into the future you deserve. You spent many years creating the old image; you need to allow yourself some time to develop the new one (but, not too much time – you *do* have a life to get on with).

At this point, it's okay to ask friends how they might describe your *best qualities*. Explain to them that this is *not* an opportunity to offer "constructive criticism," an oxymoron I just love, but rather, to help you to recognize the *good things* about yourself that you may overlook – or not even be aware of.

Once you've chosen your image adjectives, write them down on a piece of paper. Remember *my* reflection in the mirror? Well, now it's your turn! Stand in front of a full length mirror dressed as you would to go out to work or the grocery store. Say your "image adjectives" out loud. Does the reflection you're looking at mirror the adjectives you're speaking? If it does – Yea for You. You're already there image-wise and you can skip to the next Rule!

However, for many reasons, most of us do not represent ourselves as we really wish to be seen. We may follow fashion trends that are not particularly flattering to our body type; we may choose comfort over fashion to the detriment of style; or we may be caught in a time warp that would make The Flintstone's wardrobe look modern. Whatever the reason, our objective is to give as accurate and as pleasing a first impression as possible to ourselves as well as others, and our image adjectives are excellent tools.

Making the Image Change

Okay, it's time to play paper dolls. Choose a good style magazine. *Vogue, In Style, Bazaar, Glamour,* to name a few. Find pictures of clothing that match your image. Think: "Would that jacket make me look *dynamic?* Are those shoes something a *literate* person would wear?" You probably already know if that skirt will make you look fat – but will it make you look *sincere?* You know the drill. When you've chosen your new wardrobe, cut out the pictures and place them on a bulletin board – or just put them on the table. Now review to determine if you've collected fashions that will create the look you want to develop.

Next, go to your closet. Are there some things in there that fit your image already? If so, terrific; if not, don't despair. You can begin with *one new outfit*. It doesn't have to cost a fortune either – every town has at least one designer outlet or clothing discount store. Again, we're creating an *image* not an *extreme makeover*. Even if that's what you ultimately want, use *baby steps*. At the beginning of this Rule I advocate maintaining a balance. That still applies here. You are adapting your physical appearance to more accurately reflect *who and where* you are now. You are *not* trying to become an entirely different human being, you are focusing on being your best at this moment.

Once you've assembled your first outfit, put it on, and with image adjectives in hand, return to the mirror, and... look! Does the reflection give voice to the image? Does it *shout out* or maybe even *whisper* the new you? If not, don't despair. Give it another go. Remember, baby steps.

Even though this process will require *some* serious introspection, it isn't meant to be a chore. There are enough things in our lives that become "have to's." This isn't one of them.

Re-creating yourself can be a fun part of starting over, if you let it. Just imagine running into the "Ex" (if applicable) or perhaps a High School nemesis who would delight in your situation. And now, imagine leaving them wondering who that enchanting creature is. Hey – it could happen!

The main point of this exercise is to see yourself in the best possible light – allowing others to do the same.

> *"When life hands you lemons, make lemonade." I've always wondered who is going to hand me the sugar and water. Well, guess what? It's me!*

You know the adage, "When life hands you lemons, make lemonade." I've always wondered who is going to hand me the sugar and water. Well, guess what? It's me!

Rita Lee Lloyd

S.S.O.F.F. Vignettes

I have been on the most interesting journey of my life, getting married — then getting divorced! While I am much more content being in a relationship, I also realize after being the wife, cook, housekeeper, nurse, accountant, vet, and of course mother, that somewhere in this experience, it is easy to lose ourselves. We are wired to give everything to our families and usually expect very little in return. I am here to tell you balance is important for a healthy life, to be the best mom, friend and lover you can be.

> ...balance is important for a healthy life...

In the process of taking care of myself over the last three years, when it came to dating I was tempted to go back to what I was comfortable with. But now I realize I shouldn't settle for less than relationships based on respect, passion, honesty and open communication. In my short dating life, I have learned most men really do want the same thing – they just don't know how to communicate it as well as women and they can be more sensitive than us! But it's our job to let men know what we will and won't accept in a relationship – and to stick to it.

> . . . it's our job to let men know what we will and won't accept in a relationship – and to stick to it.

– *Lisa G., Ladera Ranch, California*

When my marriage ended I was living in New York City and working as a producer in various media. New York is amazing, but honestly, I missed open spaces, quiet nights, and suburbs. (Yes, I said that!)

So, I packed up and moved back out west. I quickly realized that more than a change of scenery was needed. Taking care of me had become a priority. I decided an alternative career was in order. I've always had a passion for exercise and the field of aerobics instruction and exercise science was beginning to explode. I jumped in with both feet, signing up for training, conferences, and continued education. I loved it all – and I loved how it made me feel – inside and out! I embraced my new career for years after that and I am still grateful for the joy it gives me when I step into an exercise class.

And guess what? Another benefit, I recently remarried and I'm here to tell you, I looked fabulous walking down the aisle in my wedding gown at sunset!

— Diane C., Atlanta, Georgia

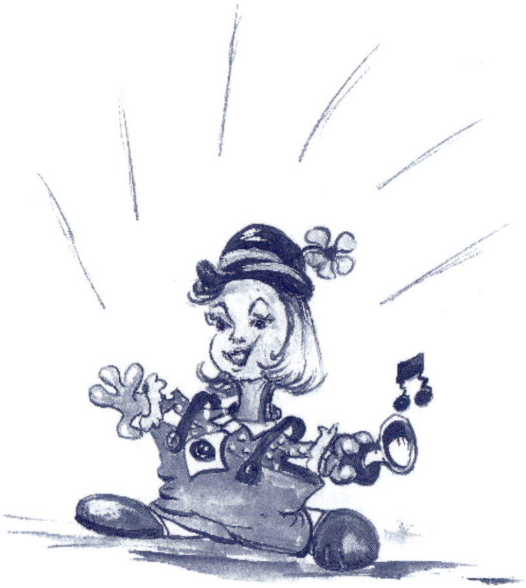

Rule #2

Keep Your Sense of Humor!

No one enjoys hearing *anyone* whine about *anything*. From birth to death the act of whining is considered by most cultures to be self-indulgent, unproductive, and just plain *annoying!* Know what? They're right!

> ... the act of whining is considered by most cultures to be self-indulgent, unproductive, and just plain annoying!

An honest expression of real emotional pain is accepted as a necessary part of healing. *However,* a whine, defined for our purpose as an "often repeated, high-pitched, plaintive, cry of distress," merely prolongs our feelings of helplessness and powerlessness and interferes with our ability to *move on,* and drives everyone else crazy! Even the most empathetic of supporters will want to run in the opposite direction the minute you open your mouth!

And, come on – we *all* know the difference between sharing our feelings and just whining. Okay – so now that we've thoroughly chastised ourselves on this issue, let's quit whining and do something about it! Laughter is the best Medicine is the advice first given in the *Reader's Digest*, circa 1934, and is still as true as ever.

The body responds in a myriad of wonderful ways to laughing.

- **Laughter is relaxing:** The whole body responds to a good belly laugh, relieving physical tension and stress.

- **Laughter can improve the immune system:** By decreasing stress hormones and increasing immune cells and antibodies, laughter improves your body's resistance to infection.
- **Laughter feels good:** When releasing the body's natural feel-good endorphins, laughter promotes a sense of well-being and can act as a temporary pain reliever.
- **Laughter is also good for the heart:** By improving the function of blood cells and increasing blood flow, laughter can help protect against a heart attack and other cardiovascular conditions.

And, while no one expects you to become a stand up comedian, being able to see the humor in difficult circumstances helps us navigate through them at a much smoother pace. Often, at seemingly inappropriate times, jokes will surface out of nowhere, some, admittedly tasteless, others downright funny, to help us alleviate the tension and move through the horrifying reality of a given situation.

> Laughter is a powerful antidote to stress, pain, and conflict.

There is a strong link between laughter and good mental health: Laughter is a powerful antidote to stress, pain, and conflict. Nothing works faster or more dependably to bring your mind and body back into balance than a good laugh. Humor lightens your burdens, inspires hope, connects you to others, and keeps you grounded, focused, and alert.

- **Laughter diffuses stressful emotions:** It's hard to feel anxious, angry, or sad when you're laughing.
- **Laughter helps you recharge your batteries:** By reducing stress and increasing energy, you are able to *stay focused longer and accomplish more.*
- **Laughter shifts perspective:** Humor allows you to see situations in a realistic, less threatening light. A change in perspective creates *psychological distance*, which can keep you from feeling overwhelmed.

Your best defense against the whines is seeing the humor in any given moment. Yes, at *this* moment, it may be impossible to see the funny side of anything. But you have the power to view things differently. Here are just a few ways to help you see this different view.

- **Laugh at *yourself*.** Admit it – sometimes you *are* funny.
- **Attempt to laugh *at* situations rather than *bemoan* them.**
- **Surround yourself with reminders to lighten up.** A "bobble head" on your dash?
- **Keep things in perspective.** Many things in life are beyond our control – especially the *behavior of other people*. While you might feel the weight of the world is on your shoulders, in the long run this perspective is unrealistic, unproductive, unhealthy, and even egotistical. Share the burden with laughter.

I've often been accused of living in denial, wearing blinders, or not being in touch with my feelings (my particular favorite). But no one will deny you're a lot more fun to be with when you keep *humor* in the equation. Both you and those who love you will *benefit* by, and *feel much better,* for it!

Suddenly Single Over Forty Female

S.S.O.F.F. Vignettes

❧

I really needed to keep my sense of humor for this – My Worst Date… Here was a guy who decided to get lunch before our date because he didn't want to spend money on lunch at the winery where we were meeting. However, he managed to eat off my plate, which I had paid for. I'm sure he's still single!

– Lisa G., Ladera Ranch, California

❧

When I first began dating again after becoming a widow, I found that not only had dating changed… there were New Rules. My first date was with a man I met through mutual friends. We spoke on the phone quite a bit before we went out. He was intelligent, good looking, owner of a thriving business – and single. I thought, "He could be a real catch!"

We went to dinner and talked all night. I couldn't wait for the next date! A few nights later, I was out with my girlfriends and he walked in with several of his friends. We all got together and had a great evening.

Before we left, he and I set up our next date for later in the week. Now, I don't know about you, but I didn't consider this evening, with everyone coming individually, a "date."

According to my math, the next date would be our second one. Apparently, according to his math, it would be our third date. Remember this point, it's important.

The following Friday, we went out for another lovely dinner. Later that evening he explained to me about the "Third Date" rule. It states; "If you don't get sex by the third date – move on!"

Well, he didn't......and I did!

I never really spoke with him again. I guess I had hurt his feelings – by breaking the rule! Oh well.

– Laura, San Clemente, California

I feel very fortunate that as a divorced over-forty-something, I could take a trip to Europe! Paris is my favorite city in the whole world. So, when in Paris, I did what Parisians do — I sat in sidewalk cafés and PRETENDED I knew how to smoke cigarettes! As you probably know, Europeans smoke like crazy and usually without filters! I personally enjoyed occasionally dragging on a Gitane, a well-known French brand, holding the cigarette between my lips and taking a fake drag on it like I was a pro. There is nothing like being at a table in a sidewalk café, watching the French parade by, and feeling like one of them.

Therefore, one day, in the presence of an adorable young Frenchman who was enjoying exchanging glances with a blonde, obviously American woman (me), I pulled a Gitane out of the box, and with flair and finesse, I placed the cigarette between my lips and lit up. With sultry eyes, I drew a breath and softly blew the smoke into the air. (Wink, wink, boy, was HE cute!) Imagine my surprise, when my girlfriend, who had accompanied me on the trip, said, "Hey, girl! You've got the wrong end of the cigarette in your mouth!" I'd still like to believe no one else noticed!

— Texas Fun Girl

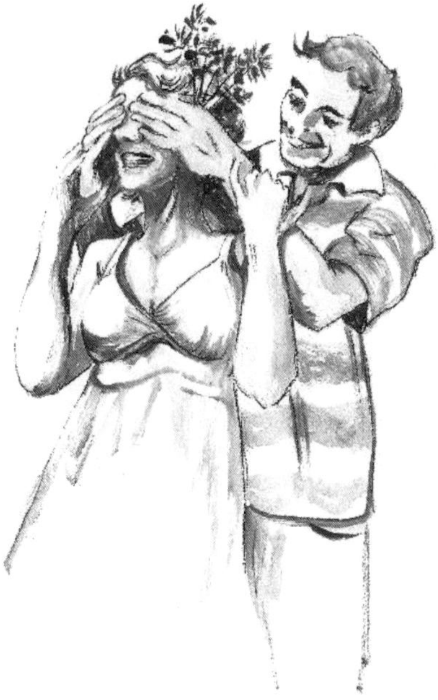

Rule #3

Date at Least One Younger Man!

There is no better morale booster than a *good flirt!* And, when it involves a younger man…… and is reciprocated…… yippee!

> There is no better morale booster than a good flirt!

Apparently, I was a "cougar" before the term became a *catch phrase* or *label* for women over forty dating much younger men. As far as I can tell, the word has been used since the late 80s, but is now acceptable in polite society and here to stay. By the way – what term is used for older men dating younger women – lucky?

Rita Lee Lloyd

We all know the "older woman/younger man" concept is nothing new. Think Patricia Neal in *Breakfast at Tiffany's* or Shelly Winters in the original *Alfie*. Or, in *real* life, Demi Moore, who prefers the term "puma." Then there is always Susan Sarandon, Goldie Hawn, and even Carol Burnett, to name a few. Not *new,* just *labeled*.

I was not familiar with the term *cougar* when I first met my younger man. In fact, I wasn't even on the prowl. But I *was* feeling discouraged, as my efforts to build a relationship with a man between forty-five and fifty-five had not yet succeeded. Obviously, a matchmaker's observation that "men in that age group were dating women half my age" wasn't far off the mark after all.

So, with my self-esteem at the level of the proverbial snake's belly, I was more than receptive to the "good flirt" previously mentioned. Suffice to say – I assumed he was younger than me, I just wasn't certain how much. And did it really matter? Not no, but *hell no*. Of course, I'd like to think that if he had been my age or older, I would still have found him as charming and delightful. But as it was, he *was* much younger, he *was* charming and delightful, and I *was* taken pleasantly by surprise. Oh, come on, I was flatout elated!

Did I believe it would *last forever?* Of course not. Did I want it to? Actually, no. It's like the line from an old song "it was too hot not to cool down." But, do I regret it even one teeny tiny moment? Absolutely not!

What this younger man did for my morale and self-esteem, not to mention other, more obvious areas, was nothing short of a miracle. If you understand and accept the reality that the *therapeutic value* of the romance outweighs the *possible repercussions*, then

> *If you understand and accept the reality that the therapeutic value of the romance outweighs the possible repercussions, then you should never have any regrets.*

you should never have any regrets. *Lots* of *lovely memories,* but *no regrets.* Imagine your favorite, most decadent chocolate dessert – with absolutely *no calories!* Honest!

Trust me and give it a try. My experience was uniquely *mine* – as yours will be *yours.*   And it may be the best dessert ever!

S.S.O.F.F. Vignettes

※

Being a Single Female Over Forty, I would say, absolutely, date a man younger than yourself! I met my "Top Gunner" at a friend's party in L.A. There he was — young, cute, smiling like Tom Cruise, and was sniffing around me. Jackpot!!! Throughout the evening I talked with several new people while he and I made occasional contact, throwing quips back and forth, stirring each other's interest. We danced for hours. Our knees started to lock. I felt like I was back in high school. Elated, care-free, and having FUN...!

A week later, he called and asked me to a funky Italian restaurant. Maybe he could only afford funk, but I liked his taste right away. We got to know each other more, and we had immediate rapport. We also had the immediate kind of animal attraction that blots out inhibitions. After dinner, he asked if I wanted to walk to the beach a few blocks away. We held hands; it felt so comfortable. We walked by the water, started to embrace and kiss. (My divorced girlfriend has a theory about kissing; "If they don't kiss well, forget it!" This one I'll never forget!) My spirited self came out so easily with him. I felt silly, giddy, and romantic. Ya know, the stuff Neil Simon would project on film.

Our relationship had excitement, wit, and as Dr. Ruth would say, "Terrrrific sex!" Eventually he moved, becoming geographically undesirable and emotionally unavailable. The sparks had been bright, and would always remain unforgettable. No regrets!

– Marla R., S.J.C, California

After my divorce, the decision to live youthfully occasionally put me in some situations that you might say were hilarious, daring, or sometimes even embarrassing. Like the time I rendezvoused with a twenty-something young man at a resort that happened to feature a water park. (But, can we talk? Just because I happened to have a bikini on hand didn't mean I thought I looked great in it!) So, there we were, bobbing around on rafts in the wave machine, and throwing ourselves down water slides on our bellies, and all I could think about was my forty-something-year-old bootie back there jiggling around for all the world (and HIM) to see! It gave a whole new meaning to the expression "Ladies first!"

— Texas Fun Girl

Rita Lee Lloyd

One of my favorite "younger man" experiences happened one year while I was celebrating New Years Eve in Las Vegas. I've noticed, every time I wear boots, great things happen. This evening I wore a purple top and black leggings with my new high-heeled black boots. I felt great! I looked good and I was with wonderful friends.

A good looking younger guy handsomely dressed in a suit, had, without me knowing, asked my friends if I was single. "Yes" they said, and before I knew it, he came from behind me, said hello, and gave me a fantastic kiss! He said I was hot and he just had to give me a kiss! Then he said that I reminded him of his mother who was from Sweden! I didn't mind the comparison because he was a man who knew what he wanted and went for it, he was hot, he was young, he was sexy, and his mother must have been beautiful, as he was so handsome!

He wanted my group to join him and his friends for drinks but we had to go. However, the event was captured by a photo and now I have created a 4x6 foot painting of "the kiss" that hangs in my living room... and I am reminded of how unexpected life can be with treats along the way!

— Marija T., Redondo Beach, California

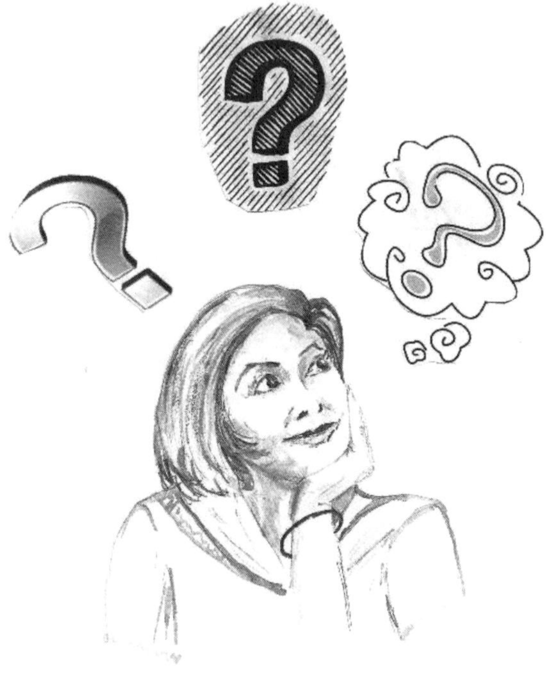

Rule #4

Never Give Your Real Age!

Okay – this statement may be a *bit* dramatic. And yes, this Rule, like the others, is based on *my* personal experiences and observations, my *perception* of *my* reality, as I have lived it.   So, at the risk of getting kicked off my soap box, here goes. . .

Why has it become so important to know an adult's age? With a few exceptions, i.e. getting your driver's license, having a health check-up, or buying cigarettes and alcohol, there is no logical reason to know a person's age *before* you even know the person. It used to be considered impolite to ask adults their age, especially ladies! That's why the euphemism, "women of a certain age" was coined – to be *polite*.

> . . . there is no logical reason to know a person's age before you even know the person.

Yes, I do feel it is rude to be asked my age by everything from the Internet (just try to join *any* new group without filling in the box marked birth date), to a membership card for a retail store. I realize, they don't personally care how old I am – they simply want the information for their demographic reports – but I really don't care to tell them.

Of course, when I was in my twenties, even thirties, I didn't think anything about giving my age. But in my forties, the reaction to my age began to change. The first time I noticed this was when an employer looked at my insurance form and commented, "Boy, I hope I look as good as you when I'm your age!" *My Age?* I was only forty-seven. Did this person, who himself was thirty-eight at the time, really think forty-seven was over-the-hill, elderly, had one foot in the grave? Regardless of why he felt it necessary to make this remark, I never felt the same around him again, and his continued joking references to my age still rankle.

The next big eye-opener occurred when a friend and I were enjoying a local street fair on a lovely afternoon. There was a booth featuring a matchmaker and my single friend suggested we take a look.

The Matchmaker was a woman in her early fifties. (I didn't ask, she volunteered.) The first question she asked *me* was my age. I told her I had just turned fifty. She was very candid and said she wouldn't be able to work with me, as men in the forty-five to fifty-five age range that I would consider "are looking for, and getting, women in their thirties."

She had been in the business for over ten years and had come to the conclusion that single women over fifty might as well get used to being *single*, unless they're willing to date an octogenarian. Or possibly move to Europe, where apparently a woman's maturity is often considered a bonus, or at the very least a non-issue. Unfortunately, that is not the norm for our culture and we need to accept it. By the way, the Matchmaker wasn't married either.

After this unexpected reality check, I looked into several other ways to meet eligible singles. In almost every instance, I had crossed the age barrier into "no (wo)mans land." In one "meet up for lunch" group, the age range for women was thirty to forty-nine, for men, thirty to sixty. Hmmmm! I have many other examples, and reasons *why*, this is my sensitive area, but suffice to say – you get the picture.

I didn't (and still don't, I hope) look as old as the calendar says. But actually *admitting* to my *real age* had become a handicap. So, what is the answer, short of lying on every form and/or to everyone I meet? Well, honesty is very important to me – but so is being accepted for *who* I am as opposed to how *old* I am. Therefore, I have chosen what I consider to be a moral compromise. A lie of omission if you will. When asked my age, I just don't tell!

> *When asked my age, I just don't tell!*

For instance, several years ago I was asked out by a business associate I had only spoken to on the phone. Prior to our date he volunteered his age and said, "May I ask how old you are?" I politely said, "No, we are both adults with grown children, so you can assume I'm not twenty. Other than that, does it really matter?" He laughed and agreed. We are friends to this day – and he still doesn't know my real age.

I know many women who gladly give their age, and if over fifty, they wear it like an "I'm six months pregnant" button at a baby shower. Well, I say – more power to you! However, I'm willing to bet, these ladies aren't in the market for a job *or* a husband at the moment. And if they are – good luck!

So please, know that this is *my* pet peeve, and it needn't become yours. *Your* experiences and your *perception* of them will be different, and I truthfully hope they are! As for me, when possible, I will continue to politely refuse to give my age when asked directly, and as for filling out forms – okay, I lie!

Rita Lee Lloyd

S.S.O.F.F. Vignettes

❧

I confess, I've always been a party girl at heart, and that hadn't changed when I found myself suddenly divorced and living alone over forty. I made up my mind then that if I had it, I'd flaunt it! So, I enjoyed some very delicious experiences while dating considerably younger men. I figured, "Hey, if they don't see me as an older woman, why should I?" Consequently, I was very quiet about my real age, and if the subject came up, I skillfully maneuvered around it. Fortunately, my body and my demeanor never gave away the lie of omission.

– Texas Fun Girl

I had never really considered my age as an issue, until I got back on the dating market. With the encouragement of friends, I signed up for an Internet dating/matchmaking service. Of course, I put down my real age and the age of the men I would like to meet. I chose to meet men who were in a range of five years older or younger than me. Well imagine my naïveté, thinking men in my own age group would want to date a woman the same age!

I received several connections, many of them my age or older. However, men in the older age group actually stated in their requirements, "women over forty need not reply!" And to top that, they had obviously posted photos of themselves that were taken ten to fifteen years earlier. So, I had two choices, give up on the Internet or start over with a younger photo of myself and lie about my age. I'm still debating my decision.

Oh, and I also received several replies from much younger men who simply wanted to date and have fun without the age requirements. But that's a story for Rule #3.

— Carol Ann, San Diego, California

Men and women have very different ways of looking at themselves, especially at their physical appearance. It's been my experience that even older, overweight men will hit on a woman and ask her age. On a scale of 1 to 10, a woman who is an 8 or 9 being asked her age by a guy who rates a -2. . . can you imagine? I mean come on!

That clearly shows us the different way men and women think. So women, start thinking like a man. . . And see that you are beautiful.

> So women, start thinking like a man. . . And see that you are beautiful.

— Marija T., Redondo Beach, California

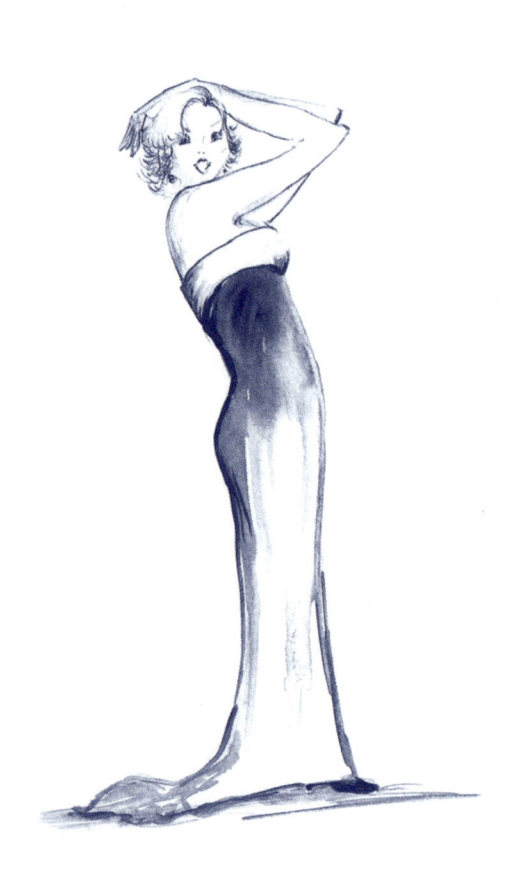

Rule #5

Live With Finesse!

Now that you've learned to take care of yourself, and you're becoming a healthy, optimistic, non-whiner, with self-esteem and humor intact, let's take a good look at your lifestyle. Remember, making the right choices begins with the *right attitude!*

> ... making the right choices begins with the right attitude!

I'm sure everyone has seen at least one 1930s movie starring Carole Lombard, Claudette Colbert, Jean Harlow, or some other "classy broad" of that era. If you haven't, rent one. Besides being fun, there may be no better example of finesse than these ladies. Webster's Dictionary defines *finesse* as the "skillful handling of a situation, adroit maneuvering, refinement." No matter how complicated their lives became, they coped with such flair, humor and elegance, you simply *had* to believe they were in complete control, and even enjoying themselves!

Admittedly, these films were popular during the Great Depression when society was so overwhelmed with reality people needed the escape they provided. Well… are you currently overwhelmed? Does your *reality* bite? Maybe a dose of finesse is what the doctor ordered!

Presenting yourself with an aura of well-being and flair does not have to put a strain on your budget. Your *income* level does not equate to your *finesse level*. Refinement and elegance are as much a state of mind as a physical image. Remember those ladies of the silver screen. Their composure was apparent whether they were in an art deco penthouse or King Kong's fist. (Faye Wray? Jessica Lange?)

> Your income level does not equate to your finesse level. Refinement and elegance are as much a state of mind as a physical image.

Another great example is a cat. Almost any cat! Ever notice how a cat can be walking along a wall, slip, scrabble back up, and keep on walking with its tail high, as though nothing happened? Or better yet, as if it *meant* to do that? Remember, "skillful handling of a situation, adroit maneuvering." Finesse!

We've all heard the advice "Act as if, fake it till you make it," Blah, blah, blah. Well, as trite as this may sound, it can and does work! I've always believed that reality is a matter of perception. *Your reality* is simply *your perception* of it. Is your glass half full or half empty? As you present yourself to others, so you will become. A skillful, adroit, refined, elegant lady, who is in complete charge of herself and her future. The woman everyone else wants to be around, to enjoy the company of. You!

> *As you present yourself to others, so you will become.*

There is a tendency in all of us to not want to appear phony, or as Grandma used to say "don't go putting on airs." Many women feel they must be humble to be appreciated. Well, I'm certainly not advocating acting like an egotistic diva. However, being confident in yourself and remaining charming in the face of adversity are qualities to which we can all aspire. Being comfortable with yourself allows others to be comfortable as well. It gives us all permission to be who we are without fear of censure. What better gift can one human being give to another?

> Being comfortable with yourself allows others to be comfortable as well.

S.S.O.F.F. Vignettes

※

I found myself single AGAIN after a second divorce, and that prompted a huge amount of soul-searching, studying and re-examining my purpose in life. It taught me that little things in life can really make a difference in how I feel about myself day to day. So, I started picking up small floral arrangements at the local market, just to add a splash of "upscale-ness" and "stopping to smell the roses" to each day. There was something about the act of placing a rose in a vase, or creating my own arrangements when I came through the door at night with a bouquet, that gave me such a sensation of being okay on my own. It didn't signify that I didn't want to try another relationship, or I didn't want to go out and date... it just gave me some happy, lilting moments of being ME. I've always sworn that a bouquet of flowers or a new chic pair of shoes is the best medicine a girl can have, especially if there isn't a significant other in the house to make out with instead!

— Diane C., Atlanta, Georgia

A few years after my divorce I'd completed my degree in Business, moved to California, and was ready for a change. All I could afford at the time was a tiny apartment in an older neighborhood. The landlord was kind enough to allow me to redecorate my new home.

I repainted every room to reflect the new me. A Roman column divided the living room from the dining area; an arch highlighted the doorway to the bedroom. Even the bathroom received faux textured walls! I bought a few large pillows to toss around and satisfy my Bohemian mood. The result was amazing – my friends complimented my ingenuity and flair.

I then summoned the courage to throw my first cocktail party, inviting friends, neighbors and co-workers. Talk about a full house. The response was overwhelmingly positive. Everyone had fun, including me. My finesse meter was off the chart and I felt better about myself than I had in years!

My personal lesson has been, when things get to be a "little too much" and fear wants to drop into my consciousness, I go into massive action. Changing the direction of what I'm focusing on changes everything and I am no longer afraid.

> Changing the direction of what I'm focusing on changes everything and I am no longer afraid.

– Marija T., Redondo Beach, California

Epilogue

I wish I could wrap this all up with the perfect pink bow… the perfect happy ending. But, honestly, this book is more about happy beginnings. **Just *surviving* after the initial impact of your personal disaster is essential. But once the dust settles you *must* move on with the rest of your life.**

Have I survived? Yes! And I have done so in good health both mentally and physically. My life is interesting and productive.

Am I still single? Yes. But I am not alone. I have a loving family and friends who support me and fill my life with unexpected joy.

Would I like to marry again? Yes! I have never closed that door. I still believe "one day my prince will come."

Following the rules for survival that I've shared with you has allowed *me* to keep hope alive. To realize I deserve to be loved and cherished, but to also realize *my* contribution to this goal. I strongly believe we *attract* what we *project*. Therefore, in our effort to "survive," we must project *our* best qualities in order to attract the best in *others*.

> . . . we attract what we project.

So I end by wishing you the perfect

"Happy Beginning!"

Acknowledgements

Words cannot express my sincere gratitude to two of the most beautiful, amazing women on this earth. Diane Y. Chapman, my friend, my mentor, without whose encouragement, guidance and expertise this book could not have become a reality. Danise L. Loftis, my friend, my lovely, patient daughter, whose love and support keeps me going, even when I don't want to.

A special thank you to Marija T. Terzic, friend and colleague, whose enthusiasm and belief in this project gave me the kick start I needed to begin my journey as an author. And a nod to my dear friend Marion Dosda, who always keeps me honest.

Rita Lee Lloyd

Special thanks as well to my many friends and fellow S.S.O.F.F.'s for sharing their personal experiences and observations, confirming the knowledge that I am not alone.

Thank you all for being in my life.

About the Author

Rita Lee Lloyd is a first-time author and a long-time survivor. After many years in the corporate world, Rita was encouraged by friends and family to share her personal experience as a Suddenly Single Over Forty Female. Surviving with style, grace and sanity intact has been a real challenge, and Rita delightfully shares her "rules" for doing so successfully. A native Californian, Rita currently lives in Orange County, California.

www.ritaleelloyd.com